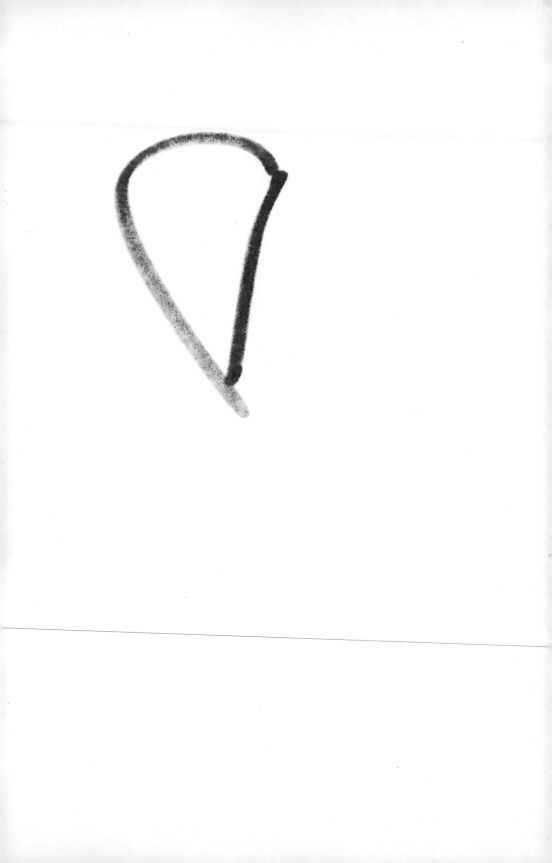

WHAT

IN THE WORLD

IS

A

HOMOPHONE?

By Leslie Presson

Illustrated by Jo-Ellen Bosson

BARRON'S

ACKNOWLEDGMENTS

A student editorial board was consulted at each stage of this book. Thank you David, Elizabeth, Giuseppe, Hunter, Jason, Kienan, Lawrence, Michael, Oliver, and Zac. Your opinions and suggestions were important and very helpful.

• •

RELATED SOURCES

Fry, Polk, and Fountoukidis. *The Reading Teacher's Book of Lists.* New York: Prentice Hall, 1984.

Merriam Webster Collegiate Dictionary, 10th ed., 1994

Random House Webster's College Dictionary, 1995.

Webster's New World Dictionary, 3rd ed., 1990.

• •

All inquiries should be addressed to:
Barron's Educational Series, Inc.
250 Wireless Boulevard
Hauppauge, NY 11788-3917

International Standard Book No. 0-8120-6585-9
Library of Congress Catalog Card No. 95-32029

Library of Congress Cataloging-in-Publication Data

Presson, Leslie.
     What in the world is a homophone? / by Leslie Presson ;
illustrated by Jo-Ellen Bosson.
        p. cm.
     Includes bibliographical references (p.).
     Summary: An illustrated dictionary that contains almost 400
pairs of pure homophones as well as separate lists of near
homophones and of contractions that are homophones.
     ISBN 0-8120-6585-9
     1. English language —Homophones—Dictionaries, Juvenile.
[1. English language—Homophones—Dictionaries.] I. Bosson,
Jo-Ellen, ill. II. Title.
PE1595.P74 1996
423'.1—dc20   95-32029
                                        CIP
                                        AC

Printed in Hong Kong
6789 6201 987654321

TABLE OF CONTENTS

INTRODUCTION

What in the world is a homophone? A homophone is a word that sounds the same as another word but has a different meaning and is spelled differently.

Homophones are also called homonyms. But homonyms include words called homographs, which are words that are always spelled the same. You don't need to choose between two or three spellings with homographs. They are spelled the same even when the words have different meanings.

Here are 387 sets of true homophones that sound alike but are not spelled the same. Choosing the right spelling for the word you want can be very important. For example, which one is good for chapped hands, a **b—a—l—m** or a **b—o—m—b**? Would **l—o—c—k—s** or **l—o—x** taste better on a bagel with cream cheese? You might walk away from a **b—o—r—e**, but you'd better run away from a **b—o—a—r**.

In various regions, people pronounce some words just a little differently. What might sound like a homophone in Indiana, Missouri, or Colorado would not be one in California or New York. These include **marry—merry, fairy—ferry, bazaar—bizarre, false—faults,** and **which—witch**. These are called near misses and are listed and defined in a separate part of this book. You could make your own pictures for the near misses.

HOW TO USE THIS DICTIONARY

This dictionary will help you identify the word you wish to spell or need to define. Each colorful illustration makes it easy to choose the right homophone. However, even homophones can have more than one meaning. The definition that is illustrated appears first. Read the complete definition to determine all the other meanings.

The homophones appear in alphabetical order. You'll find **bare— bear** after **bard—barred**, but not again after **be—bee**. If the homophones begin with different letters like **ceiling—sealing**, you'll find them first under *C* and again under *S*. The names of people and countries have not been included. Slang has been avoided. "Contractions" that are homophones can be found on page 187 before "Near Misses." When you find two spellings for one word like **bootee** and **bootie**, both are equally correct.

The same word can be a noun, a verb, and an adjective. *A*, *an*, and *the* are used before the definitions for most nouns. *To*, *did*, and the endings *ed* and *ing* are used with verbs or action words.

Care was taken to select words that are used every day, including a few foreign words. You will discover some that are new to you. If you can't find a word that you think is a homophone, check all the pages for that letter and then the list of "Near Misses" starting on page 189.

Words are wonderful tools that help us communicate. They can be toys as well. Make up a silly sentence using a pair of homophones. Homophones can make comical rhymes, too. Play with them.

With **pride** they **pried** a **bare bear** from its lair.
That **grizzly** was **grisly. They're** no longer **there**.

A

ad - an advertisement

add - to combine, increase

adieu - good-bye; a farewell

ado - a fuss, trouble

aerie - an eagle's nest; a high stronghold

airy - breezy, light

ail - to be sick; to have trouble or pain

ale - a drink

air - a breeze; gases surrounding the earth

heir - one who inherits

aisle - the passageway between rows of seats

isle - an island

all - every one, the whole

awl - a small pointed tool

allowed - permitted, provided

aloud - out loud; loudly

altar - a place for worship

alter - to change

ant - a small insect

aunt - a female relative

arc - a curved line; an arch

ark - a vessel; a chest

ascent - a rising or climb up; an upward slope

assent - to agree, consent

assistance - help, aid

assistants - the helpers, the aides

ate - did eat

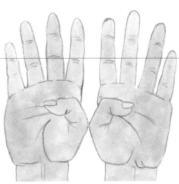

eight - the number after seven

attendance - the number present; paying attention

attendants - people who serve or are present

aural - sense of hearing; of the ear

oral - spoken; of the mouth

axes - large, chopping tools

axis - a central line about which an object rotates or is arranged

aye - yes; always

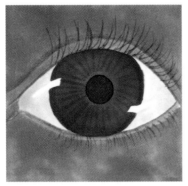

eye - the organ of sight

I - the personal pronoun meaning yourself

B

bail - a payment or security to get out of jail until trial; to remove water; to jump out

bale - a large bundle; to make into bales

baited - tormented; lured; tempted; harassed

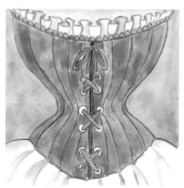

bated - held in, reduced

bald - hairless; plain or blunt

bawled - has cried aloud; was scolded

ball - any round body; a formal dance

bawl - to cry aloud; to scold

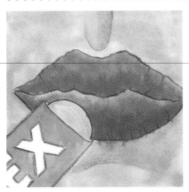

balm - a soothing ointment

bomb - an explosive; to attack

band - a group; a strip or ring of metal, cloth, wood, or rubber; to join together

banned - forbidden; condemned

bard - a poet

barred - fitted with bars; excluded

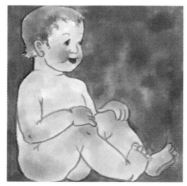

bare - naked; empty; simple

bear - an animal; to carry; to endure; to produce

B

baron - a nobleman or magnate

barren - without plants; sterile; boring

base - one of four markers on the baseball field; the foundation or principal part; low

bass - a singer or musical instrument with a deep, low range

based - founded on; headquartered

baste - to moisten while cooking; to join with loose stitches

be - to happen; to live; to continue

bee - the insect that makes honey

beach - a sandy shore; to ground a boat on land

beech - a hardwood tree

beat - to whip; to defeat; to pound or punish; to move up and down; a rhythm in music

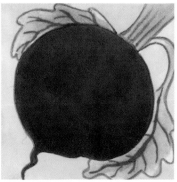

beet - a dark red vegetable

beau - a boyfriend, sweetheart

bow - a knot; a device to shoot arrows; to play a stringed instrument; curved

been - was, past of *be*

bin - a storage box

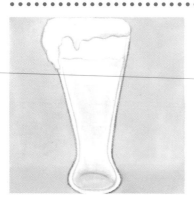

beer - an alcoholic drink

bier - a platform for a coffin

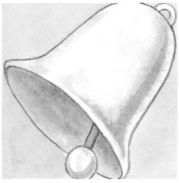

bell - a cuplike object that rings

belle - a popular female

berry - a small fruit

bury - to cover or put away out of sight

berth - a bunk; a ship's mooring; an assigned place

birth - being born; to create; to bring forth; the origin

billed - charged; gave a statement

build - to erect; to establish; to create; to develop

blew - did blow, spouted

blue - the color; gloomy

bloc - a political group; a

block - a city square; a solid piece; to obstruct

boar - a wild hog

bore - to drill a hole; a dull person

board - a flat piece of wood; to get onto; a governing group; the meals provided with lodging

bored - uninterested; drilled

boarder - one who gets onto; a lodger

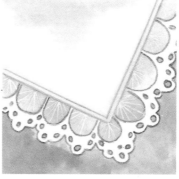

border - an edging; the dividing line; a narrow strip

bold - fearless, daring; steep; clear

bowled - rolled a bowling ball; moved swiftly; astonished

bolder - more bold

boulder - a large rock

bootee, bootie - a soft, knitted shoe

booty - the loot; spoils of war

born - brought into life; created

borne - carried; endured

borough - a section of New York City; a town

burro - a small donkey

burrow - an animal's home; to dig

bough - a main branch of a tree or shrub

bow - to bend in respect; the front part of a ship

braid - three or more strands interwoven; a trimming; to interweave

brayed - made the loud cry of a donkey

brake - a device to slow down and stop

break - to crack; to burst; a fracture; to disrupt; a sudden change

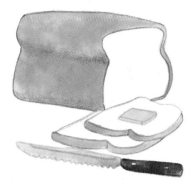

bread - a baked food

bred - mated; raised, trained

brewed - steeped; fermented

brood - a flock; offspring; to dwell on sad feelings

brews - steeps; ferments

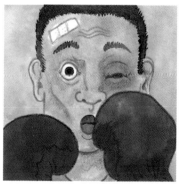

bruise - a surface injury; to hurt

bridal - of a bride or wedding

bridle - a head harness for a horse; to control or restrain

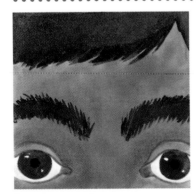

broach - to risk capsizing; to start a discussion

brooch - a large pin with a clasp

brows - eyebrows; foreheads; the edges of a cliff or hill

browse - to nibble; to examine casually

but - yet, except, still

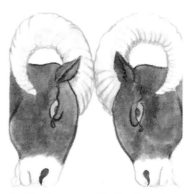

butt - to ram with the head; the thick end; the object of jokes; to join end to end

buy - to purchase

by - near; at; during; not later than

bye - good-bye

C

cache - a hiding place; hidden supplies

cash - money

caddie - a golfer's attendant

caddy - a small tea container

callous - unfeeling

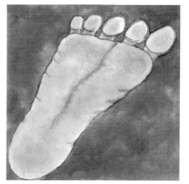

callus - a thick, hard place on the skin

canon - a church law

cannon - a large piece of artillery

canter - a smooth, moderate gallop

cantor - a singer in a synagogue

canvas - a firmly woven cloth

canvass - a survey; to solicit

capital - an uppercase letter; the top of a column; the seat of government; invested money

capitol - the building in which government meets

carat, karat - a gem's weight; the purity of gold

carrot - an orange vegetable

carol - a Christmas song; to sing

carrel - a small alcove for study

cast - a rigid dressing for a broken bone; actors in a play; to mold; to vote; to throw; to assign a role

caste - social rank

cede - to grant or yield

seed - a part of a plant; the sperm of an animal; to sow

ceiling - the top part of a room; the upper limit

sealing - shutting tight; hunting seals; the closing

cell - a small prison room; a small part of a living thing; a small unit

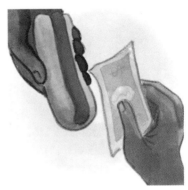

sell - to exchange for money

cellar - a basement; a space below the ground

seller - one who sells things

censor - a critic who prohibits

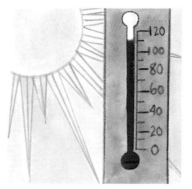

sensor - a device to detect and measure

cent - a penny coin

scent - a smell; to perfume

sent - transmitted; caused to go; drove

cereal - a grain used for food

serial - in a series; continuing regularly

cession - a giving up, yielding

session - a meeting

chance - luck; an opportunity; a gamble; an accident

chants - sings; a monotonous rhythm

chased - pursued, followed; hunted

chaste - pure, modest, simple

cheap - inexpensive; contemptible

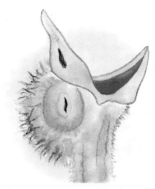

cheep - a young bird's call

chews - bites and grinds with the teeth

choose - to select; to decide; to prefer

chic - fashionably elegant

sheik - an Arab chief

chili - a hot pepper or stew

chilly - moderately cold; unfriendly

choir - a group of singers; a part of a church

quire - 24 sheets of paper

choral - sung by a chorus

coral - hard skeletons of marine growth; a color

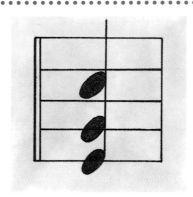

chord - musical notes played together

cord - a thick string; a measure of logs; a rib in fabric

cored - took from the center

chute - a trough down which to slide or drop

shoot - to discharge; to wound; to move swiftly; to photograph

cite - to summon to a court; to quote; to mention

sight - a view; to look carefully; vision

site - the location or scene

clause - a group of words that contains a noun and verb; a part of a document

claws - sharp nails or pincers; scratches; tears

close - to shut, stop, or block

clothes - garments; covers with clothing

coarse - rough; common

course - a place to golf; the route; an instruction; a part of a meal

coffer - a treasure chest

cougher - one who coughs

colonel - a military officer

kernel - the seed of corn; the inner part of a nut; the most important part

complement - to make complete; that which perfects

compliment - to praise; a courteous act

C

council - a group of people called together for discussion

counsel - advice; a lawyer; to advise

core - the center; the inner or most important part

corps - a group of people working together

coward - one who lacks courage, is shamefully afraid

cowered - cringed from cold or fear; crouched

creak - to make a squeaking sound

creek - a small stream

crewel - a soft yarn used in embroidery

cruel - mean, causing pain and suffering

crews - groups of people working together

cruise - to voyage; a vacation on a ship; to move at an even speed

cue - a long rod; a signal or hint

queue - to wait in line; a pigtail

currant - a small raisin or sour berry

current - a flow of water, air, or electricity; in the present

cygnet - a young swan

signet - an official seal

cymbal - a musical instrument

symbol - a sign or token; a mark or letter

● ●

D

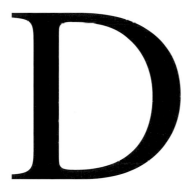

dam - a barrier to hold back water; an animal mother

damn - a curse; to condemn

days - the plural of *day*

daze - to stun; a state of shock

dear - beloved; costly

deer - a woodland animal

dense - thick, compact

dents - marks on the surface

desert - to leave behind; to abandon

dessert - the last part of a meal

D

dew - droplets of mist

do - to act; to finish; to put forth

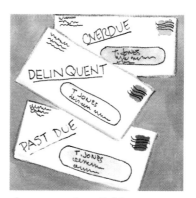

due - owed; suitable; expected

die - to stop living; to end; a shaping tool

dye - to color or tint; a coloring

47

disburse - to pay out

disperse - to scatter; to disband; to break up

discreet - careful, prudent

discrete - separate, distinct

doe - a female deer or rabbit

dough - a flour mixture for baking

does - the plural of *doe*

doze - to nap; a light sleep

done - finished; performed

dun - a dull grayish color; to ask for payment of a debt

dual - double, twofold

duel - an arranged fight between two armed persons

dyeing - to color with dye   **dying** - expiring; ending

• •

E

earn - to gain by labor

urn - a vase

eave - the lower edge of a roof

eve - the day before a holiday; the evening

eek - a sound made in surprise

eke - to barely manage

. . . .

eight - the number after seven

ate - did eat

. . . .

ewe - a female sheep

yew - an evergreen tree

you - a personal pronoun

• •

ewes - female sheep

use - to put into service; to employ; to treat; to consume

yews - evergreen trees

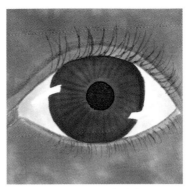

eye - the organ of sight

aye - yes; always

I - the personal pronoun meaning yourself

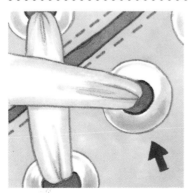

eyelet - a small hole

islet - a little island

F

faint - weak; timid; to swoon

feint - a pretended attack

fair - a bazaar; lovely; clear; honest; blonde

fare - the price or fee; food

faun - a Roman deity, half goat-half man

fawn - a young deer; to show delight like a dog

faze - to disturb

phase - a time period; to adjust

feat - a notable deed

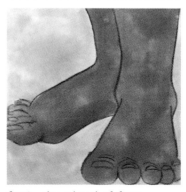

feet - the plural of *foot*

fined - charged money; punished

find - to discover; to locate; to decide

fir - an evergreen tree

fur - soft, thick animal hair

fisher - a large marten; one who fishes

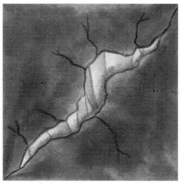

fissure - a crack or cleft

flair - a sense of style; a talent; ability

flare - to blaze up; to curve out; a signal light; an outburst

flea - an insect

flee - to run away

flew - did fly; escaped

flu - an illness

flue - a chimney pipe

floe - floating ice

flow - to pour out; to glide;
the movement of a liquid

flour - ground grain

flower - a blossom; to reach the best stage

F

• •

foaled - gave birth to a colt or filly

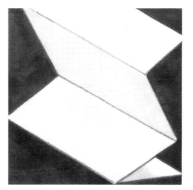

fold - to double over; to wrap; a pen for sheep

• •

for - directed to; in order to; because of

fore - in the front

four - one more than three

foreword - a preface

forward - toward the front; bold

forth - forward; onward

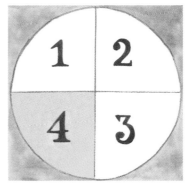

fourth - after third, before fifth

F

foul - filthy; bad; wicked; stormy; to entangle; to hit outside the limits

fowl - birds used for food; any bird

franc - foreign money

frank - honest; open

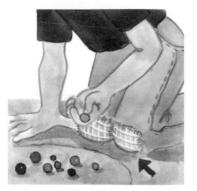

frays - wears out, makes ragged; small battles

phrase - a group of words, not a clause or sentence

frees - releases; clears

freeze - to become frozen; to stop

frieze - a decorative panel

friar - a member of a religious order

fryer - a chicken; a pan for frying

F

G

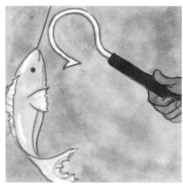

gaff - a large hook on a pole for landing fish

gaffe - a social blunder

gait - pace; manner of walking

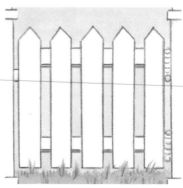

gate - the door in a fence

gamble - to bet; to take a risk

gambol - to frolic, skip about

G

genes - genetic units

jeans - denim pants

gibe - to taunt; a jeer

jibe - a sudden shift in direction; to be in accord

gild - to coat with gold

guild - an association of people

gilt - a thin coating of gold

guilt - the blame for a wrongdoing

gnu - an antelope

knew - did understand;
remembered

new - fresh; for the first time

gofer - an errand runner

gopher - a small animal

gorilla - a large ape

guerrilla, guerilla - a soldier not in the regular army

gourd - the fruit of a plant

gored - pierced by an animal's horn

grate - to shred; to make a harsh sound; a metal grille

great - large; fine; notable; important

grill - to broil; to question; broiled food; a restaurant

grille - an open framework of metal

grisly - horrible, ghastly

grizzly - the bear

groan - a deep sigh; to moan

grown - increased; matured

guessed - supposed; estimated

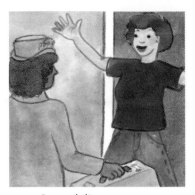

guest - a visitor

guise - appearance; style of dress

guys - the plural of *guy*; ropes

H

hail - ice pellets; to greet; to salute

hale - healthy, vigorous

hair - a threadlike growth; a very small degree

hare - a hopping animal

hall - a passageway; a large room

haul - to drag, move by pulling

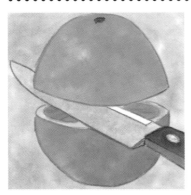

halve - to divide in half

have - to own, possess; to get; to permit; to experience

handsome - good-looking

hansom - a carriage

hangar - a garage for planes

hanger - a holder

H

hart - a male deer

heart - a symbol of love; an organ of the body; the hub or center

hay - dried plant stalks

hey - a call to get attention

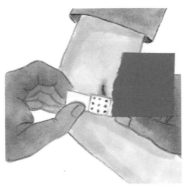

heal - to cure or mend

heel - a part of the foot or shoe; a scoundrel; an end slice of bread

hear - to listen to

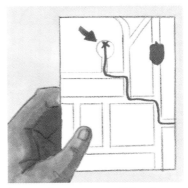

here - in, at, or on this place

heard - did hear

herd - to move together; a group

heir - one who inherits

air - a breeze; gases surrounding the earth; an attitude

heroin - a narcotic drug

heroine - a female hero

hew - to chop down; to conform

hue - a tint of a color; an outcry

hi - an informal greeting

high - having a great height; tall; lofty; elevated; exhalted

him - that man

hymn - a sacred song

ho - a cry to get attention

hoe - a tool for weeding

hoard - to store; a hidden supply

horde - a swarm; a crowd

H

hoarse - having a rough, husky voice

horse - the animal

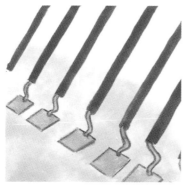

hoes - tools for weeding

hose - tubing; stockings

hole - a cavity; an opening

whole - intact; complete; healthy

holy - sacred; pure

wholly - entirely, completely; fully; totally

hostel - an inn

hostile - unfriendly

hour - sixty minutes

our - belonging to us

H

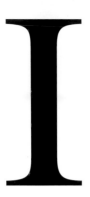

I

I - the personal pronoun
meaning yourself

aye - yes; always

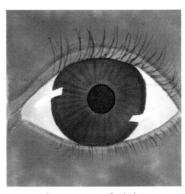

eye - the organ of sight

idle - inactive; useless

idol - an object of worship

in - inside; within

inn - a hotel or tavern

incidence - the rate of occurrence

incidents - the events

intense - very strong

intents - future plans

isle - an island

aisle - the passageway between rows of seats

islet - a little island

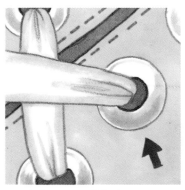

eyelet - a small hole

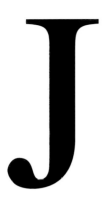

jam - a fruit spread; to crowd; congested traffic

jamb - the side post of a doorway

jeans - denim pants

genes - genetic units

jibe - a sudden shift in direction; to be in accord

gibe - to taunt; a jeer

• •

K

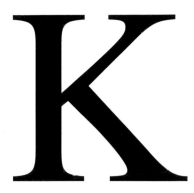

kernel - the seed of corn; the inner part of a nut; the most important part

colonel - a military officer

knave - a dishonest person; a rascal

nave - the main part of a church

knead - to work dough

kneed - struck with a knee

need - to want; to require

knew - did understand; remembered

gnu - an antelope

new - fresh; for the first time

K

knight - a rank or title of honor

night - a time of darkness

knit - to loop yarn; to join together; to wrinkle the brow

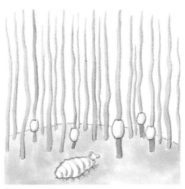

nit - an insect egg

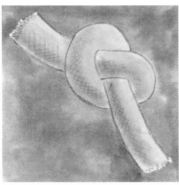

knot - to tie; a tight fastening; a lump in wood; a nautical mile

not - in no way

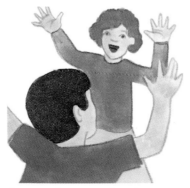

know - to recognize; to understand

no - not any; not so; not at all

knows - understands; recognizes

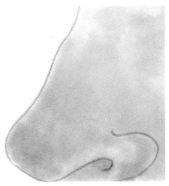

nose - a part of the face; the sense of smell

K

L

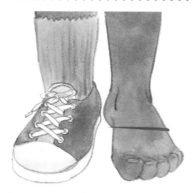

lacks - needs; wants; to be short of

lax - loose, slack

lain - did lie down; rested; remained

lane - a narrow road; the route

lama - a Tibetan monk

llama - an animal native to the Andes Mountains

laps - drinks; overlaps; gentle splashes; parts of a race

lapse - a small error; a passing of time

lay - to place; did lie down

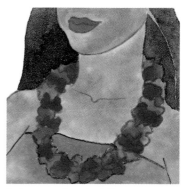

lei - a garland of flowers

L

leach - to dissolve and wash away

leech - a bloodsucking worm

lead - a heavy metal

led - guided; directed

leak - an accidental escape; to let out

leek - an onionlike vegetable

lean - to bend or rest against; thin

lien - a legal claim on another's property for payment of a debt

leased - rented

least - smallest or slightest

L

lessen - to decrease, make less

lesson - something learned

levee - an embankment; a dike

levy - to fine or collect; a tax

lie - to tell a falsehood; to recline; an untruth

lye - a strong, alkaline substance

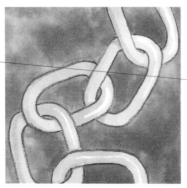

links - loops of a chain; connects; a golf course

lynx - a wildcat

lo - look! see!

low - not high or tall; deep; mean

load - a burden; a large amount; to transfer

lode - a metal deposit in the earth; a rich supply

L

loan - to lend; what was borrowed

lone - alone; apart; single

locks - devices for securing; gates for changing water depth; jams together; curls of hair

lox - smoked salmon; rocket fuel

· ·

loot - to plunder; stolen goods

lute - an old stringed instrument

· ·

M

made - prepared; created; did; caused; reached

maid - a servant; a young woman

mail - postal material; to send; the fabric of a knight's armor

male - the masculine sex

main - the most important part; the ocean

mane - the long hair on an animal's neck

maize - corn

maze - a confusing network

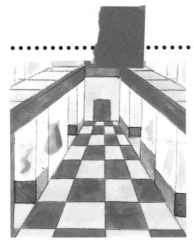

mall - a shopping center; a shaded walk

maul - a heavy mallet; to injure, handle roughly

manner - a way of acting; a method

manor - the main house on an estate; the estate

mantel - the shelf above or the front of a fireplace

mantle - a cloak; to cover

M

marshal, marshall - a sheriff; a military commander; to lead

martial - warlike

mask - a covering for the face; to hide

masque - a fancy costume party

massed - gathered in a large group

mast - a tall upright pole

meat - food; the edible part of a nut

meet - to be introduced; to assemble; to be present; to fulfill

mete - to pass out, distribute

M

medal - an award, usually metal

meddle - to interfere

metal - an element like gold, iron, brass, or copper

mettle - courage; spirit

mewl - to cry like a newborn baby

mule - the animal offspring of a mare and a donkey

mews - cats' cries; British stables

muse - to meditate; to reflect; a goddess of the arts

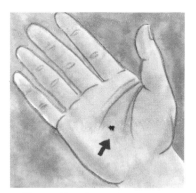

might - power; strength; may

mite - a tiny insect; a very small creature or amount

mince - to cut in small pieces; to act very daintily

mints - candies; herbs; places where a government makes money

M

mind - to obey; memory; thought; to care

mined - dug from the earth

miner - a worker in a mine

minor - a juvenile person

missal - a book of prayers

missile - a weapon fired toward a target

missed - failed to hit, meet, do, attend, see, or hear

mist - to spray with water; a thin fog; water vapor

moan - a low, sad cry; to complain

mown - was cut down

moose - a large animal

mousse - a light, airy food

M

morning - the first part of the day

mourning - showing grief

muscle - strength; an organ of the body

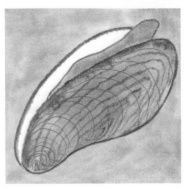

mussel - a shellfish

mustard - a spicy yellow condiment; a plant with yellow flowers

mustered - enlisted; assembled; gathered

N

naval - of or for a navy

navel - a belly button

nave - the main part of a church

knave - a dishonest person; a rascal

nay - no; a negative vote

neigh - the whinny of a horse

need - to want; to require

knead - to work dough

kneed - struck with a knee

new - fresh; for the first time

gnu - an antelope

knew - did understand; remembered

nicks - small dents or wounds; injures slightly

nix - to veto; no

night - a time of darkness

knight - a rank or title of honor

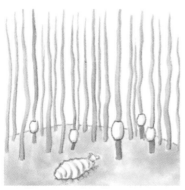

nit - an insect egg

knit - to loop yarn; to join together; to wrinkle the brow

no - not any; not so; not at all

know - to recognize; to understand

none - no one, not any, not at all

nun - a woman in a religious order

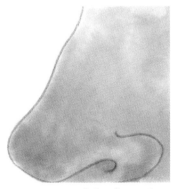

nose - a part of the face; the sense of smell

knows - understands; recognizes

N

not - in no way

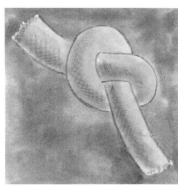

knot - to tie; a tight fastening; a lump in wood; a nautical mile

oar - long-handled paddle

or - a word giving a choice of two

ore - minerals

ode - a lyric poem

owed - was indebted

oh - a cry of surprise or pain

owe - to be in debt

O

one - a single thing; united; the same

won - did win

oral - spoken; of the mouth

aural - sense of hearing; of the ear

our - belonging to us

hour - sixty minutes; the time of day

P

paced - walked back and forth; measured the speed

paste - an adhesive; to stick on

packed - placed things together; crammed; packaged

pact - an agreement; a contract

pail - a bucket

pale - lacking color; a fence picket

pain - suffering; to hurt

pane - a section of window glass

pair - two of a kind; a couple

pare - to peel; to cut, trim

pear - the fruit or tree

P

palette - a painter's board for mixing colors

pallet - a thin bed on the floor; a platform

passed - went by; moved forward or through

past - time gone by; history

patience - calm endurance

patients - those getting medical care

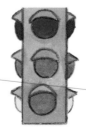

pause - a brief stop; to hesitate

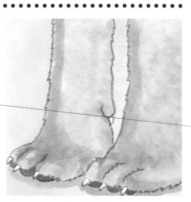

paws - animals' feet; touches roughly

peace - quiet; freedom from war; a state of harmony

piece - a part; a section or an example

peak - the high point, the top

P

peek - a quick look

pique - anger; to offend

peal - a loud ringing sound

peel - the skin or rind; to pare

pearl - a precious bead

purl - a knitting stitch

pedal - a foot lever; to press with the feet

peddle - to move about and sell things

peer - to look closely; an equal; a British nobleman

pier - a long dock; a column

phase - a time period; to adjust

faze - to disturb

P

because of the rain,

phrase - a group of words, not a complete clause or sentence

frays - wears out, makes ragged; small battles

plain - simple; clear

plane - an aircraft; a flat surface; a woodworking tool

plait - a braid of hair; to braid

plate - a shallow dish; to cover with metal

pleas - appeals; excuses; requests; entreaties

please - to satisfy; a polite request

plum - the fruit; a tree; a rewarding job

plumb - in a straight line; to probe; a lead weight

pole - a tall, round stick; an opposing point

poll - a place to vote; to gather opinions

P

pore - to study carefully; a tiny opening

pour - to flow freely; to rain heavily

praise - to commend; strong approval

prays - implores; asks in prayer

preys - hunts for food; robs or kills

presence - a dignified appearance; being present

presents - gifts

pride - self-esteem; great satisfaction

pried - extracted with difficulty; snooped

pries - wedges open; snoops

prize - a reward; to value highly

P

primer - an elementary textbook

primmer - more prim, very proper

prince - a king's son

prints - marks; designs; writes; impressions

principal - foremost; the head of a school; the amount of a debt

principle - a basic truth; a rule of law or ethics

profit - financial gain; to benefit

prophet - one who predicts the future

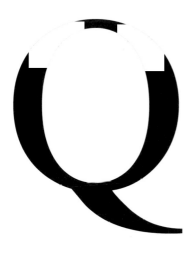

quarts - liquid amounts of 32 ounces

quartz - rock crystal

Q

queue - to wait in line; a pigtail

cue - a long rod; a signal or hint

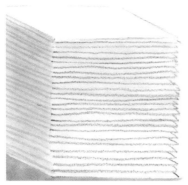

quire - 24 sheets of paper

choir - a group of singers; a part of a church

· ·

R

rabbet - to make cuts; a groove in wood

rabbit - a long-eared animal

R

rain - drops of water; to pour down

rein - a leather strap; to curb

reign - to rule

raise - to lift; to increase; to collect; to cause to grow

rays - shafts of light; large flat fishes

raze - to demolish, tear down

rap - a tap or knock; to strike; to blame; a fast vocal

wrap - an outer covering; to enclose; to wind or fold

rapped - struck with quick blows

rapt - engrossed; carried away by emotion

wrapped - covered; enclosed

real - true; actual

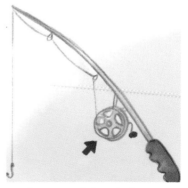

reel - a spool; to wind up, whirl, or stagger

red - a primary color

read - learned from printed words; understood

reed - a tall, thin grass; a musical instrument

read - to utter printed words; to gain information from print

R

reek - a strong smell; to stink

wreak - to inflict damage; to express anger

residence - a place where one lives

residents - people who live in a place; doctors in training

rest - to lean or relax; to sleep; what is left

wrest - to pull or force away with a twist

retch - to try to vomit

wretch - a miserable person

review - an inspection; to go over again; a report; to evaluate

revue - a musical show with dancing and skits

● ●

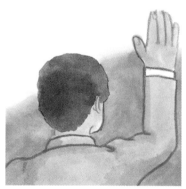

right - correct; fitting; the opposite of left; a legal privilege

rite - a ritual; a ceremony

write - to form words, letters, books; to compose

ring - a piece of jewelry; to make a sound; to encircle

wring - to squeeze and twist

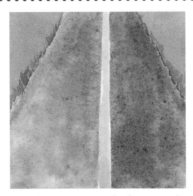

road - a way made for travel

rode - did ride

rowed - did go in a boat with oars

roe - fish eggs

row - in a line; to propel by oars

role - a part to act

roll - a small portion of bread; to move; to turn over; to form a ball

R

roomer - one who rents a room

rumor - gossip

root - the underground part of a plant; a cause; a basic part

route - a road or course for travel

rose - the flower; did rise

rows - uses oars; orderly lines

rote - by habit; memorized

wrote - did write

rouse - to stir up, excite; to wake

rows - noisy quarrels

rude - impolite; crude

rued - was sorry, regretted

R

rung - did ring; the step of a ladder or chair

wrung - twisted

rye - a grain

wry - distorted; ironic

S

sac - a pouch in a plant or an animal

sack - a soft bag; to plunder

sail - a part to catch the wind; to glide smoothly; to navigate on water

sale - a special offering at reduced prices; an exchange for money

sane - sound of mind; sensible

seine - a fish net; to fish with a net

saver - a person who saves or avoids waste

savor - to enjoy; a special taste or smell

scene - the setting; a place; a part of a play or film

seen - looked; viewed; visited; observed

scent - a smell; to perfume

cent - a penny coin

sent - transmitted; caused to go; drove

scull - a racing shell; to use an oar from side to side

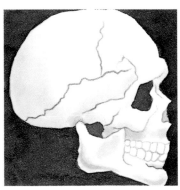
skull - the bones of the head

sea - the ocean

see - to look; to understand; to find out

sealing - shutting tight; hunting seals; the closing

ceiling - the top part of a room; the upper limit

seam - the place where two parts are joined together

seem - to appear; to look like

seas - bodies of water

sees - looks; understands; finds out

seize - to grab; to take control; to bind

seed - a part of a plant; the sperm of an animal; to sow

cede - to grant or yield

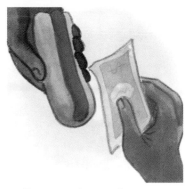

sell - to exchange for money

cell - a small prison room; a small part of a living thing; a small unit

seller - one who sells things

cellar - a basement; a space below the ground

sensor - a device to detect and measure

censor - a critic who prohibits

serf - a slave to a landowner

surf - to ride on the crest of a wave; breaking waves

serge - a fabric; to finish the edge of cloth

surge - a large wave; a sudden increase in intensity

serial - in a series; continuing regularly

cereal - a grain used for food

S

session - a meeting

cession - a giving up, yielding

sew - to stitch; to mend; to make

so - in order that; very; likewise; therefore; also

sow - to scatter seeds

shear - to clip; to trim

sheer - extremely steep; very thin; to turn aside

sheik - an Arab chief

chic - fashionably elegant

shoe - a foot covering; a horseshoe

shoo - to drive away; begone!

S

shone - glowed; stood out

shown - did show; exhibited

shoot - to discharge; to wound; to move swiftly; to photograph

chute - a trough down which to slide or drop

sic - to cause to attack

sick - ill; very disturbed

side - the edge or surface; either half

sighed - did sigh; breathed deeply and audibly

sighs - deep loud breaths

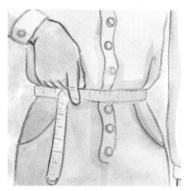

size - the measurement, bulk, dimension; to stiffen

S

sight - a view; to look carefully; vision

cite - to summon to a court; to quote; to mention

site - the location or scene

signet - an official seal

cygnet - a young swan

slay - to murder or kill

sleigh - a vehicle on runners

sleight - skill with tricks

slight - thin, small, light; to neglect or snub

soar - to rise high; to fly like a bird

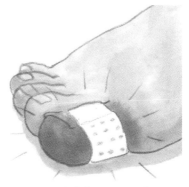

sore - painful; annoyed

S

soared - flew like a bird; rose high

sword - a weapon with a long sharp blade

sole - the bottom of a foot or shoe; one and only; a fish

soul - the spirit; the vital part; a person

soled - supplied with a shoe's bottom

sold - did sell

some - a portion

sum - the total

son - a male offspring

sun - the bright center of the solar system

staid - proper; sober; sedate

stayed - remained; propped up; stopped the action of a court

S

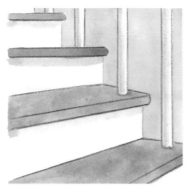

stairs - steps

stares - fixed looks

stake - a pointed post; a wager; a share; to gamble; to mark

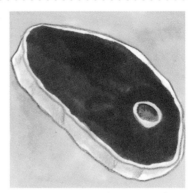

steak - a slice of meat or fish

stationary - fixed; motionless; unchanging

stationery - writing paper and envelopes

steal - to rob; to smuggle; to move or act secretly

steel - a hard metal

step - a stair; a single movement

steppe - a broad plain

stile - a set of steps over a fence

style - a manner; the fashion; to design

S

straight - even; direct; honest

strait - a narrow waterway

succor - aid; to help

sucker - a lollipop; a victim; a new shoot of a plant; a part used for sucking

suite - connected rooms; a set of furniture

sweet - sugary; pleasant; kind

symbol - a sign or token; a mark or letter

cymbal - a musical instrument

T

tacked - pinned; changed course

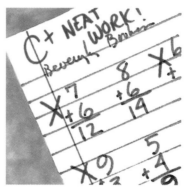

tact - sensitivity; skill in saying the right thing

tacks - small nails; pins

tax - a payment; a burden; to levy

tail - at the hind end; to follow

tale - a story

taper - a thin candle; to lessen

tapir - a large, hoglike animal

taught - educated; did teach

taut - tightly stretched

T

tea - a drink; an afternoon party

tee - a small golf peg; the place to start playing golf

team - two or more horses; a group working or playing together

teem - to swarm

tear - a salty drop from the eye

tier - a row of seats

teas - drinks made from soaking leaves from plants

tease - to mock; to torment

tense - strained; feeling or showing tension

tents - shelters made of canvas

tern - a seabird

turn - to rotate; to wrench; to move around; to change; a chance

T

their - belonging to them

there - in or at that place

threw - tossed; upset; sent rapidly

through - from end to end; finished

throes - spasms of pain or struggles

throws - sends rapidly; pitches

throne - a ruler's chair; a king's power

thrown - have, has, or was pitched

thyme - a minty herb

time - a measure of duration; every moment, past and future; a set period

tic - a twitch; a spasm

tick - a clicking sound; a small blood-sucking insect

T

tide - the rise and fall of the seas; a current

tied - bound; fastened

to - toward; because; until; along with; so as to

too - more than enough; also

two - the number after one

toad - amphibious animal

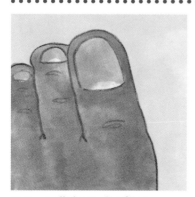

toed - having toes

towed - pulled

toe - a digit on the foot

tow - to pull or drag

T

told - informed; said

tolled - rang slowly

tracked - followed; traced

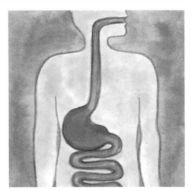

tract - a system of body parts; a stretch of land; a political paper

troop - a unit of scouts or soldiers; to walk together

troupe - a group of singers or actors; to travel as a group

trussed - supported; tied up

trust - confidence; hope; care

T

U

undo - to untie; to do away with; to ruin

undue - too much; improper

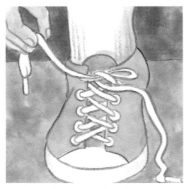

urn - a vase

earn - to gain by labor

use - to put into service, to employ; to treat; to consume

ewes - female sheep

yews - evergreen trees with needles

U

V

vain - proud; conceited; worthless

vane - a wind direction indicator

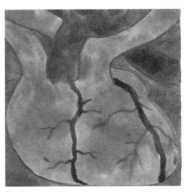

vein - a blood vessel

vale - a valley

veil - a light fabric cover; to hide or conceal

vice - an evil habit or conduct; a fault or failing

vise, vice - a device that holds firmly

V

W

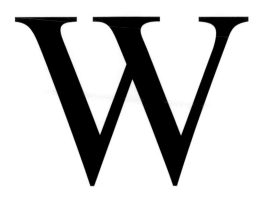

wade - to walk through water; to proceed with difficulty

weighed - measured the weight; chose carefully

waist - a part of the body; a vest

waste - left over, unusable; to ruin, squander, wear away

wait - to be ready; to stay for; to serve food

weight - a heavy object; the amount of heaviness or importance

waive - to excuse, give up, defer

wave - to move back and forth; an upsurge; an ocean swell

wares - merchandise for sale; pottery

wears - on the body; bears use; holds up

W

warn - to caution; to tell of coming danger

worn - used as clothing; shows use; exhausted

way - road; path; course; method

weigh - to measure heaviness; to choose carefully

we - persons speaking or writing

wee - tiny; very early

weak - lacking strength; feeble

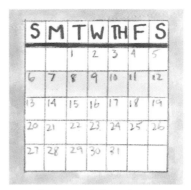

week - seven days in a row

whole - intact; complete; healthy

hole - a cavity; an opening

wholly - entirely, completely; fully; totally

holy - sacred; pure

W

won - did win

one - a single thing; united; the same

wood - lumber; timber

would - is, are, or was willing; could

wrap - an outer covering; to enclose; to wind or fold

rap - a tap or knock; to strike; to blame; a fast vocal

wrapped - covered; enclosed

rapped - struck with quick blows

rapt - engrossed; carried away by emotion

wreak - to inflict damage; to express anger

reek - a strong smell; to stink

W

wrest - to pull or force away with a twist

rest - to lean or relax; to sleep; what is left

wretch - a miserable person

retch - to try to vomit

wring - to squeeze and twist

ring - a piece of jewelry; to make a sound; to encircle

write - to form words, letters, books; to compose

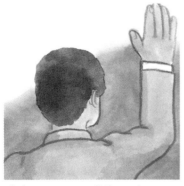

right - correct; fitting; the opposite of left; a legal privilege

rite - a ritual; a ceremony

wrote - did write

rote - by habit; memorized

W

wrung - twisted

rung - did ring; the step of a ladder or chair

wry - distorted; ironic

rye - a grain

Y

yew - an evergreen tree

ewe - a female sheep

you - a personal pronoun

yews - evergreen trees with needles

ewes - female sheep

use - to put into service; to employ; to treat, to consume

yoke - a wooden harness for oxen; bondage

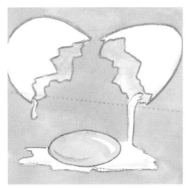

yolk - the yellow part of an egg

CONTRACTIONS
THAT ARE HOMOPHONES

he'd - he had, he would

heed - to pay attention; take notice

he'll - he will, he shall

heal - to cure or mend

heel - part of the foot; a scoundrel; the end slice of a loaf of bread

here's - here is, here has

hears - listens

I'll - I will, I shall

aisle - a passageway

isle - an island

it's - it is, it has

its - that which belongs to it

there's - there is, there has

theirs - belonging to them

they're - they are

their - belonging to, made by, or done by them

there - in that place

we'd - we had, we would

weed - a plant that grows wild

we'll - we will; we shall

wheel - a round turning device

we've - we have

weave - to interlace, make, spin

who's - who is, who has

whose - belonging to whom

you'll - you will

yule - the season of Christmas

you're - you are

your - belonging to or done by you

NEAR MISSES

accept - to take or receive something; to admit someone

except - to leave out, exclude

acclamation - applause

acclimation - used to the climate

affect - to influence; to stir feelings

effect - the result of a cause

all ready - entirely ready, prepared

already - previously; so soon

all ways - every way possible

always - all the time; forever

any one - any single person or thing from a group

anyone - anybody; any person at all

any way - in any manner at all

anyway - regardless; in any case

bases - important places; foundations; headquarters

basis - a principal or fundamental part

bazaar - a marketplace; a benefit sale

bizarre - strange, odd, fantastic

confidant - a person with whom secrets are shared

confident - sure of oneself; assured of success

descent - a coming or going down; ancestry; a downward slope

dissent - to disagree; a disagreement

elicit - to draw forth; to call for an answer

illicit - unlawful; improper

emigrate - to leave one's native land

immigrate - to settle in a new country

eminent - famous; important; outstanding

imminent - about to happen, impending

every one - every single person or thing named

everyone - everybody, all of them

fairy - a tiny elf with magical powers

ferry - a boat used to cross; to transport

false - untrue

faults - defects; misdeeds; blames

fate - destiny; one's fortune or final outcome

fete - a festival; to honor

graham - whole wheat

gram - a small unit of metric weight

incite - to arouse, urge to action

insight - an understanding

lair - an animal's den

layer - a single thickness

liar - one who tells lies

lyre - a small ancient harp

lightening - making lighter; becoming brighter

lightning - a flash of light

marry - to wed, join, unite

merry - joyful, lively, full of fun

pistil - part of a flower

pistol - a small firearm

rancor - bitter resentment

ranker - smellier; coarser

receipt - a written record

reseat - to seat again

than - a word used to compare two things

then - at that time; next; in that case

trustee - a person who manages for another's benefit

trusty - dependable, reliable

vary - to change, alter, make different

very - extremely, truly, really

verses - lines of poetry; lyrics of a song; a stanza

versus - against; in contrast with

vial - a small glass bottle

vile - wicked; disgusting

waddle - to walk like a duck

wattle - the flesh on the neck of a turkey; a mud and straw mixture

wail - to make a loud, long cry of grief or pain; a mournful cry

whale - a large sea mammal

wear - to have on; to show; to impair by use; to irritate

where - in, at, or from what place

weather - conditions of temperature, wind, and humidity; to survive

whether - in either case

were - the past of *to be*

whir - to spin with a vibrating sound

wet - damp; to add water

whet - to sharpen

which - what one; that one

witch - a sorceress; an ugly, old woman

while - a period of time; during that time

wile - a sly trick

whine - to complain; a high-pitched sound

wine - a drink made from grapes

whither - where; to what place

wither - to fade; to dry up